- Bonelli's eagle feather
- Ruffed grouse feather
- Common quail egg
- House spa[rrow]
- Northern cardinal feather
- Wedge-tailed eagle feather
- Northern gannet feather
- Domestic chicken down feather
- Blue and yellow macaw feather
- Peacock feather
- Meadowlark egg

GW01481633

For Tharu and all the kids of the world. Go outside. Play, look up, and imagine a world where all of us can be happy together.

– N.P

For Marc and Mel, who have accompanied me in the wonderful world of birds during our excursions through forests and mountains. And Bruna, because I hope to be able to teach and guide you in the spectacular and wild nature of this world.

– M.G

First edition published in 2026 by Flying Eye Books Ltd.
27 Westgate Street, London, E8 3RL, UK
www.flyingeyebooks.com

Represented by: Abrams & Chronicle Books c/o Media Participations
57 rue Gaston Tessier, CS 50061
75166 Paris Cedex 19, France

https://www.media-participations.com/en/subsidiaries
productsafety@abramsandchronicle.co.uk

Text © Nadeem Perera and illustrations © Montse Galbany 2026

Nadeem Perera and Montse Galbany have asserted their rights under the Copyright, Designs and Patents Act, 1988, to be identified as the Author and Illustrator of this Work. All rights reserved. No part of this publication may be reproduced or transmitted in any form or by any means, electronic or mechanical, including photocopying, recording or by any information and storage retrieval system, without prior written consent from the publisher.
No part of this book may be used or reproduced in any manner for the purpose of training artificial intelligence technologies or systems. Flying Eye Books Ltd expressly reserves *What Makes a Bird?* from the text and data mining exception, in accordance with Article 4 of European Parliament Directive (EU) 2019/790.

Edited by Christina Webb
Designed by Maisy Ruffels

1 3 5 7 9 10 8 6 4 2

Published in the US by Flying Eye Books Ltd.
Printed in China on FSC® certified paper.
ISBN: 978-1-83874-206-5

WHAT MAKES A BIRD?

An Illustrated Guide to the Bird World

Nadeem Perera

Montse Galbany

FLYING EYE BOOKS

Contents

08 What Makes a Bird?
10 A Bird's Body
12 Bird Evolution
14 Take Flight
16 Flightless Birds
18 Birdsong
20 Plumages
22 *Fact File:* Feathers
24 Bird's Eye View
26 *Fact File:* Eyes
28 Beaks and Bills
30 *Fact File:* Beaks

32 Where Do Birds Live?
34 Oceans
36 Mountains
38 Woodland
40 Deserts
42 Polar Regions
44 Cities
48 Rainforests

50 What Do Birds Do?
52 Coupling Up
54 Killer Strategies
56 Epic Journeys
58 *Fact File:* Navigation
60 Nesting
62 *Fact File:* Nests
64 Nature's Gardeners
66 Night Vision

68 Becoming a Birder
69 Where to Start
70 Identify a Bird
72 Make a Bird Log
74 How You Can Help

76 Glossary & Index

Introduction

In every climate, on every continent, birds abound. From thick rainforest canopies to city skyscrapers, birds have adapted to every habitat on Earth since the time of the dinosaurs. Some go on epic journeys while others stay in the same area their whole lives. There are those that weave nests, species that use their beaks as tools, and even birds with glow-in-the-dark night vision. Join us as we journey through the majestic, skilful, and surprising behaviours of the bird world.

What Makes a Bird?

All birds have wings (whether or not they can fly) and all birds have beaks, feathers, and two legs. But what else makes a bird?

The smallest bird in the world is the **Cuban bee hummingbird**, a mere 6.2 cm (2.5 inches) long. Its eggs are the size of coffee beans!

A Bird's Body

All birds have feathers, and they're the only animals that grow them. Their bodies have lots of other special features too...

Light bones
Birds don't have heavy bones. This makes it easier for them to move and fly around.

Bald eagle

Strength
Most birds can fly. They have strong muscles in their wings and chest that help them take off.

Feathers
Birds have feathers that help them stay warm, and in most cases, help them fly.

Laying eggs
Birds lay eggs, often in a nest, and baby birds grow inside them until they're ready to hatch.

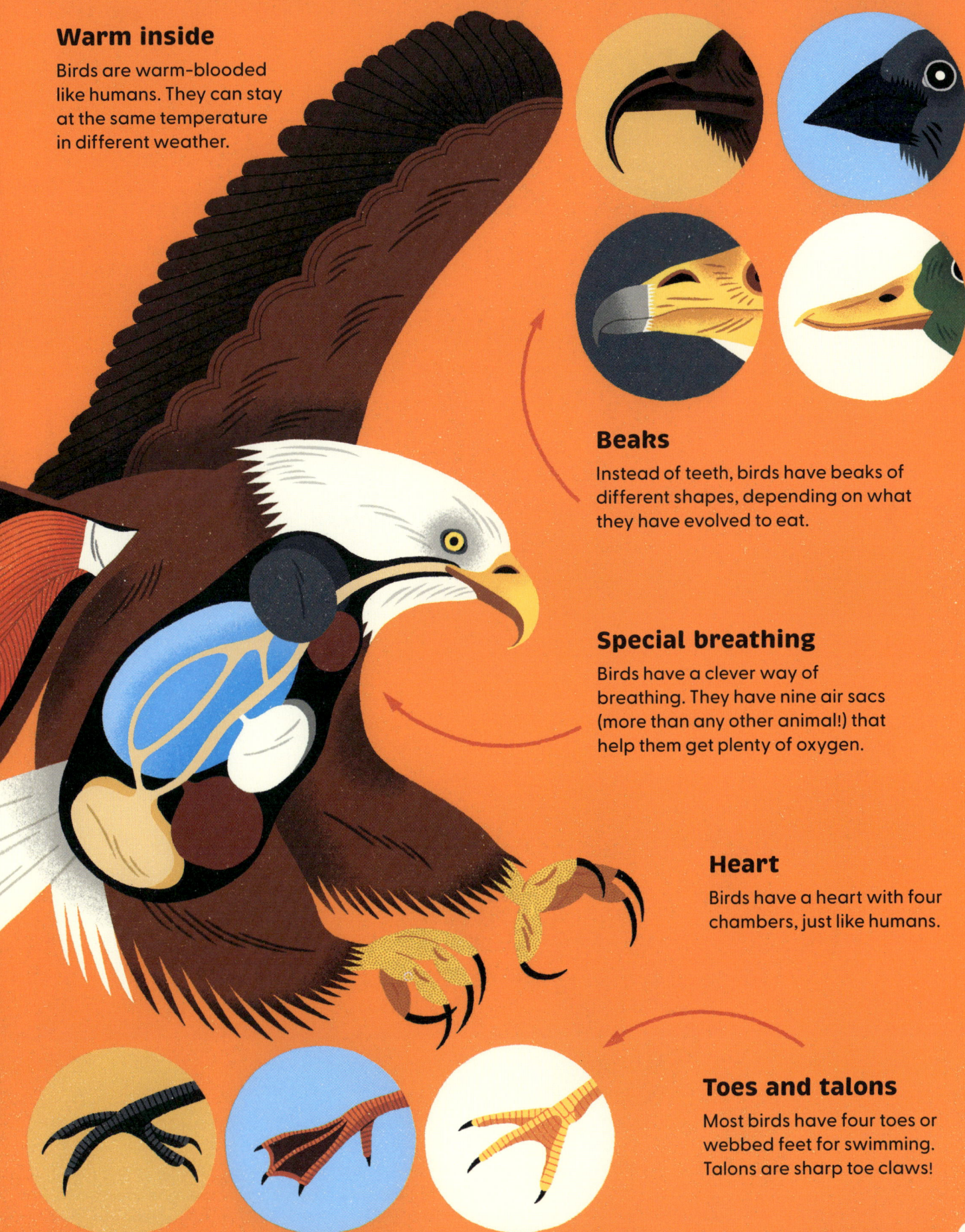

Warm inside
Birds are warm-blooded like humans. They can stay at the same temperature in different weather.

Beaks
Instead of teeth, birds have beaks of different shapes, depending on what they have evolved to eat.

Special breathing
Birds have a clever way of breathing. They have nine air sacs (more than any other animal!) that help them get plenty of oxygen.

Heart
Birds have a heart with four chambers, just like humans.

Toes and talons
Most birds have four toes or webbed feet for swimming. Talons are sharp toe claws!

Bird Evolution

When did birdlife begin? One of the first birds ever recorded by scientists lived during the time of dinosaurs, around 150 million years ago.

Allosaurus

Coelurus

Many dinosaurs had feathers or hair all over their body. But only some dinosaurs had wings and could fly.

Archaeopteryx

Being able to fly meant they could better find food and escape danger.

Dinosaur extinction

Flying probably saved birds from extinction 66 million years ago. All dinosaurs went extinct except feathered therapods, which eventually became the 10,000 species of birds we see today.

Ancient bird species

Some birds have hardly changed since prehistoric times, and have managed to avoid extinction over millions of years without having to completely evolve.

Having evolved 20 million years ago, **African ostriches** are one of the oldest living bird species. They have survived because they are big, strong, and speedy.

Hoatzin

Sandhill crane

Ostriches are the largest birds on Earth. They have long, muscly legs perfect for sprinting to escape predators!

Take Flight

Birds have light bones full of space for air, which makes it easier for them to fly. Oxygen-rich blood flows through their bodies, giving them the energy for long flights.

Flying V

Canada geese fly together in a V-shape. Each bird flies a little above and behind the bird in front of them, which makes it easier and quicker to fly against the wind.

Head in the clouds

The **common swift** appears in Europe in the summer, after travelling more than 17,700 km (nearly 11,000 miles) from southern Africa. They spend more than 99% of the time in the air without needing to touch ground!

Flocking together

A group or gathering of birds is known as a 'flock'. There is safety in numbers, and synchronised flight formations make it easier for birds to travel longer distances.

Starlings fly in a 'murmuration' – a flock with as many as six million individuals! The birds gracefully dance across the sky together as one big mass, forming giant dotted patterns in the sky.

European starlings perform this mesmerising spectacle at dusk during autumn and winter.

Scientists aren't sure why starlings form murmurations, but the constant movement might be a way of confusing and throwing off predators.

White stork

Swallow

Bohemian waxwing

Barnacle goose

Flightless Birds

Even though they all have feathers, not all birds fly. Flightless birds evolved to run or swim instead to suit their lifestyles.

Emperor penguin

Diving birds
Some birds, like penguins, have heavier bones to help them dive deep down under the water to catch their food.

Flightless birds

Some birds can't fly because they lack the right muscles in their chests, so they have other ways to hunt, travel, and escape predators.

Kākāpō

Kiwi

Piercing eyes

The **cassowary** lives in the rainforests of Australia and New Guinea. They never needed to develop the ability to fly.

They are the heaviest birds in the world, and pretty threatening!

Razor-sharp 5-inch talons.

Penguin

Emu

Because Oceania separated from other continents so long ago, its animals evolved uniquely, and there aren't many predators. Cassowaries have become apex predators (animals at the top of the food chain) – instead of having to fly to flee from predators or find food, they grew large and strong.

Birdsong

Birds are admired for their chirpy singing all over the world. Have you ever wondered how, when, and why they make such beautiful sounds?

Dawn chorus

Birds sing just before or as the sun rises, in what's known as the 'dawn chorus'. Each bird has a set role and order, like a choir. If you wake up early you can hear it yourself!

European robin

Voice box

Humans have a larynx (voice box) with one air passage, while birds have two. This means they can make two sounds at once. That'd be like you speaking two sentences at the same time!

Human larynx

Bird voice box

Plumages

Every species of bird has feathers. They can be silky, fluffy, stripy, spotty, colourful, and cleverly camouflaged. There are wing, tail, and waterproof plumages – and ones just for showing off!

Blue jay

True blue

Blue birds aren't truly blue. Their feathers absorb all colours except blue, which scatters and is what we see. If you rotate a blue jay's feather, the blue may disappear, revealing dark brown feathers instead!

Gentoo penguin

Bird of many feathers

Penguins are a type of bird that swim instead of fly. Their short, waterproof feathers are tightly packed, to aid swimming and keep warm as they spend up to 75% of their time in cold water.

Courtship displays

In the bird world, looks really do matter! Many birds perform a feather display to attract a mate. The more extravagant the ritual, the more good-looking they seem.

Bird of paradise

Bowerbird

The male Indian peafowl, a **peacock**, has one of the most impressive courtship displays. It raises its shimmering jewel-like feathers to dazzle a potential mate.

1 The peacock faces a peahen, lifts its 2-metre-long (6.56 feet) train and splays out its feathers to create a huge fan.

2 They give them a shake, creating a rustling sound and vibrating about 25 times per second! This is known as 'train-rattling'.

3 **Peahens** will decide to mate with the peacocks with the best feathers and displays. If a male's feathers look healthy and are still intact, it's a good sign that he hasn't run into much trouble.

Ruff

Frigatebird

FACT FILE
Feathers

Feathers help give some birds the ability to fly, but there is a lot more to them than catching wind. They help birds communicate, camouflage, keep them warm, and scare away predators.

The **Australian tawny frogmouth** is nocturnal, so it camouflages well in trees while sleeping during the day.

Some birds have clumps of feathers on their heads called 'crests', used to show when the bird is excited, threatened, or curious.

Cockatoo

Owls have special feathers on their faces called 'bristle feathers' that help direct sound to their ears.

Short-eared owl

Cygnets (baby swans) hatch with grey feathers. They turn brown, then greyish, and finally white when fully grown.

There are birds that produce a waterproof oil that they apply to their feathers – using their beaks!

Mallard

Soft down feathers help keep baby birds warm by trapping air, but they can't be used to fly.

Turkey chick

Bird's Eye View

Bird vision is often 'overlooked'! But they have the largest eyes for their size of any animal besides frogs. Many birds have an excellent sense of smell and eyesight.

Golden eagle

Red grouse

Eagle Eyed

An eagle's vision is among the sharpest in the animal kingdom, allowing them to spot prey from 3.2 km (about 2 miles) away. Despite eagles being smaller than humans, their eyes are roughly the same size as ours!

All birds have a third eyelid. This helps protect them from sunlight, even while looking directly into the sun.

Night sight

UV (ultraviolet) light rays from the sun are invisible to humans, but visible to birds! About half of all bird species can see UV trails on nectar, trees, and plants, helping them find food.

The human eye has three cones for colour vision. Birds, like the **common kestrel**, have a fourth cone for seeing UV light.

Bird vision

Human vision

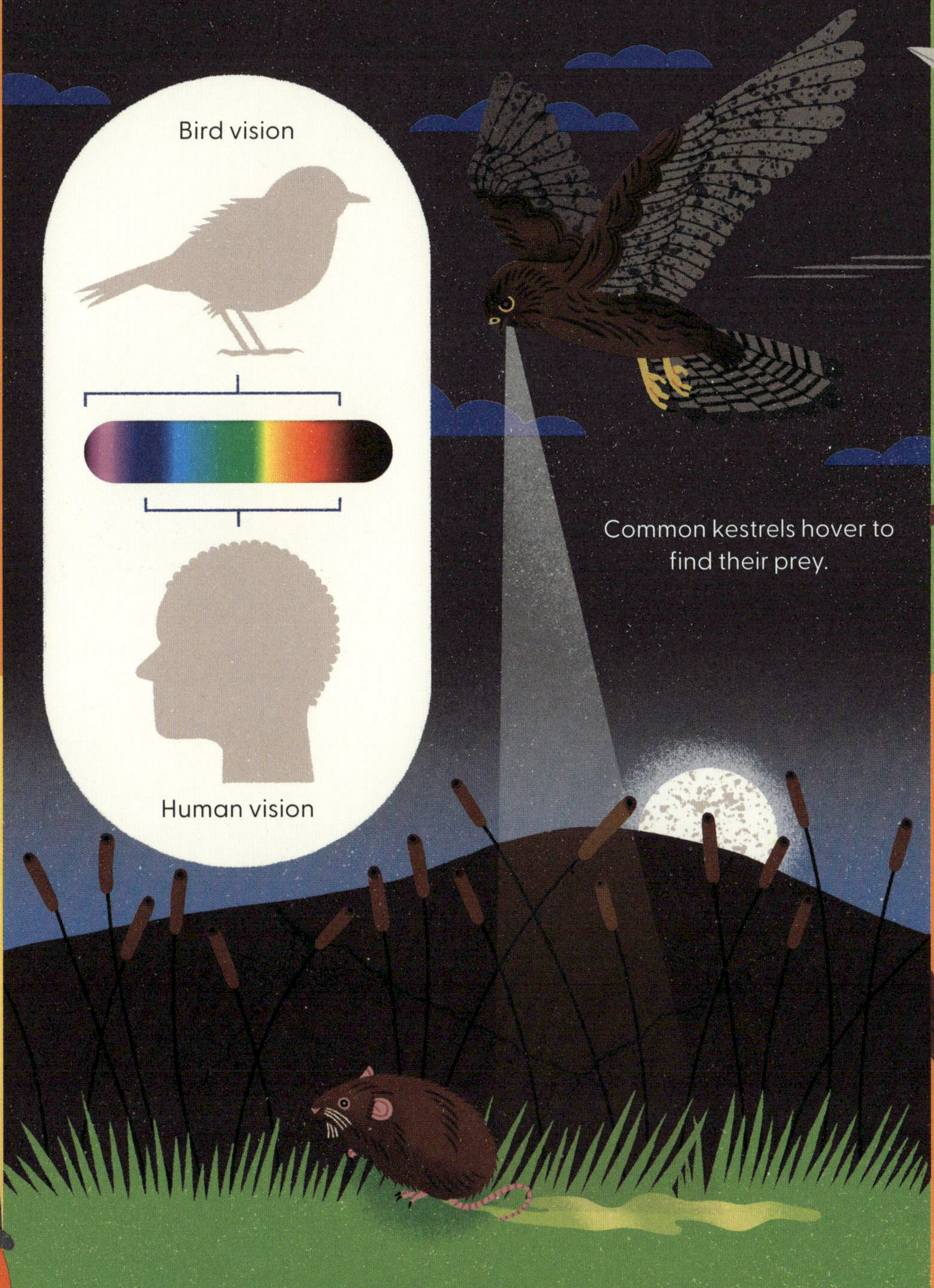

Common kestrels hover to find their prey.

Kestrels use their vision to spot urine trails from small mammals, which glow under UV light. They can follow these trails straight to their next meal!

Australian magpie

Blue tit

African grey parrot

Budgerigar

FACT FILE
Eyes

What's it like to have a bird's eye view of the world? Here are some fascinating and surprising facts about avian eyesight.

Burrowing owl

Barn owl

Owls can't move their eyeballs. This helps keep their vision steady.

Great horned owl

Short-eared owl

Some birds, like nightjars, have oil droplets in their eyes that help them filter light so they can hunt at night.

Nightjar

Parrots are some of the only birds that sleep deeply like humans, which means they might have dreams!

Scarlet macaw

Potoos have slits in their eyelids that allow them to detect movement even when their eyes are closed!

Hawks generally have eyes on the sides of their head, but can see forwards, too.

Red-tailed hawk

Beaks and Bills

A key feature of a bird is its beak, and many beaks are unique. Different types give us clues about each bird's behaviour, diet, and lifestyle.

Sharp and soft

Waterbirds like ducks use their smooth, flat beaks and teeth filters to sift through water and mud to find little creatures to eat.

Australasian shoveler

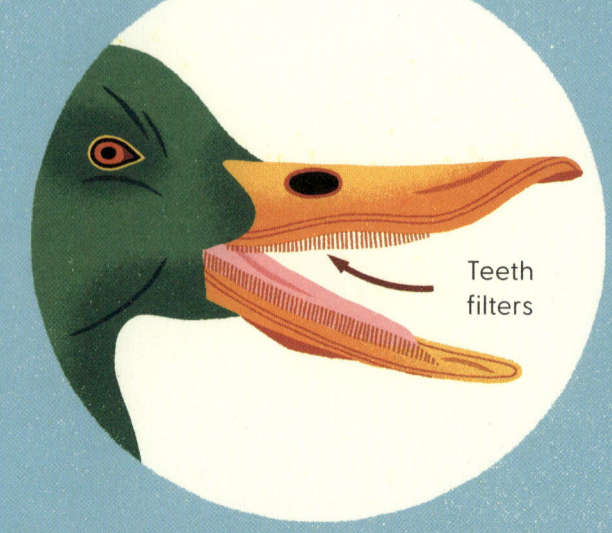

Teeth filters

Darwin's finches

On the Galápagos Islands, Charles Darwin discovered that finches of the same species had evolved different beaks to suit the food they ate on each island!

Unique beaks

Unusual or oversized beaks are often a sign of a bird's particular lifestyle and diet.

Long-billed curlew

Great spotted woodpecker

Crossbills live in coniferous forests. Their beaks are specially designed to eat the seed pods that grow in the trees!

Baby crossbills are born with regular-shaped beaks, but then their bill begins to twist and cross over at the tips.

A crossed bill helps the birds pry open pinecones to reach the seeds inside. They wedge their beaks into the cone scales, then twist to open it.

Toucan

Spoonbill

FACT FILE
Beaks

Beaks are an essential part of being a bird. From powerful dagger-like beaks to flat rounded spoons and pin-like thin bills, each beak serves a purpose.

Pelicans catch lots of fish at once with huge expanding pouches underneath their beaks, which can store three times more fish than their stomach!

American white pelican

Panama yellow-headed Amazon parrot

The outer layers of beaks are made of keratin (the same stuff as human nails) and can also grow back if damaged.

Bird beaks don't just include the bird's mouth but its nose, too!

Emden goose

Woodpeckers have strong, pointed chisel-like beaks for hammering holes into wood so they can reach food like tree sap or insects.

Pileated woodpecker

Toco toucan

The edges of a toucan's huge beak are serrated like the edges of a knife. This tool helps them slice through rainforest fruits with hard skin.

Where Do Birds Live?

Different species of birds show that they handle whatever the planet throws at them. Penguins flourish in icy waters, wallcreepers conquer mountain faces, and pigeons colonise cities.

Oceans

Ocean birds must be quick-thinking and fast-moving. Birds that brave the seas tackle strong winds, crashing waves, and big beasts.

Below

Most aquatic birds, like **gannets**, use their webbed feet as a rudder, to steer them in the right directions underwater. Bird swimming speeds need to match that of the fish they want to catch.

Above

Seabirds, like the **Manx shearwater**, are fast and have good eyesight so they can catch prey near the surface of the ever-moving current. They twist and turn in the air to avoid sharks and seals.

Wandering albatross

Albatrosses are masters of the seas. They are fantastic navigators, and can spend up to five years at sea, without visiting land. The wandering albatross has huge wings, 3.5 metres (11.5 feet) wide, that help it use the wind to glide over the open ocean.

Fulmar

Some birds such as fulmars, albatrosses, and petrels are called 'tubenoses' due to their tube-shaped nostrils which have a special filter that removes salt from seawater so that they can drink it.

King penguin

Birds that brave the deep have eyes that can see underwater. Below the waves, king penguins' pupils expand more than any other bird's to let in more light when they dive to dark depths of 300 metres (984 feet).

Mountains

Mountains can be harsh habitats for birds. They must brave high altitudes, rugged terrain, and scarce food. Against the odds, birds find ways to make unforgiving peaks work to their advantage.

Raven

Upper and lower middle

Corvids and **falcons** inhabit the upper middle; owls occupy the lower middle. They can be found at the base, but prefer the peace and quiet up here!

Himalayan bulbul

Grandala

Himalayan wood owl

Base

In the foothills of the Himalayas, you can spot the bright blue grandala, the bulbul, and the fluffy collared **falconet**.

Peak

There is less oxygen at the top. **Bearded vultures** can handle low air supplies, and eat what other birds consider 'waste'. Bones make up to 90% of their diet!

Wallcreepers are tiny birds that live in crevices in mountain faces. They use their long beaks to find insects scuttling within the rocks.

Golden eagles are the most dominant mountain birds. In Mongolia, Kazakh eagle hunters have used them to hunt prey during winter for centuries.

Woodland

When you think of where birds live, woodlands are the most obvious habitat. But lots of other animals also live in trees, so birds must compete for food, shelter, and territory.

Treetops and skies

Birds of prey, such as buzzards, **goshawks**, and **kites**, can be seen soaring above woodlands. They use forests for nesting but hunt far and wide.

European honey buzzard

Tree trunks

Tree-dwelling birds like chickadees, **treecreepers**, waxwings, and **great spotted woodpeckers** rely on berries, insect larvae, and tree holes for survival. Their small size helps them thrive above the leaf litter.

Chickadee

Waxwing

Goshawks and other forest raptors have wide, short wings that make them nimble for moving between trees.

American robin

Eurasian wren

Forest floor
Brave birds such as wrens, **blackbirds**, American robins, and green woodpeckers risk running into residents such as foxes, wildcats, and snakes. Fallen leaves and fungi are used to build nests, while insects make the perfect meal.

Green woodpecker

Woodpeckers drill holes in trees to make nests that predators cannot easily get to, or to find larvae that is hidden beneath the tree bark.

Deserts

Deserts are tough places to live, with scorching hot temperatures and little water to drink or plants to eat. Birds here must find clever ways to survive.

Egyptian vulture

Shrubland and desert flats

Roadrunners and hummingbirds live among trees in North American deserts. Hummingbirds feed on insects, nectar, and cactus fruit such as prickly pears. Roadrunners eat lizards and snakes.

Roadrunner

Mongolian ground jay

Steppe

Mongolian ground jays and hoopoes live in the dry, grassy plains and forests, known as steppes, of the large, cold Gobi Desert in Mongolia and China.

Mountains and rocky plateaus

Desert vultures have evolved to 'scavenge' – feed on dead animals. This might seem gross, but getting rid of decaying flesh helps prevent disease from spreading through the desert.

Black-chinned hummingbird

Eurasian hoopoe

The **Rüppell's vulture**, of sub-Saharan Africa, is the highest-flying bird. It soars up to 11,000 metres (6.8 miles) high. That's roughly 30 Empire State buildings! Up here, it can scan for food.

Owls don't only live in the woods. Tiny **burrowing owls** live in underground dens to keep safe and cool in North and South American deserts.

Polar Regions

The North and South poles see constant daylight in summer and no sunrise in winter. Their birds must cope with snow, ice, strong wings, and freezing climates. So how do they survive?

Adélie penguin

Tundra Arctic

Though the **Arctic redpoll** is miniature in size and weighs less than a chocolate bar, it can endure Arctic tundra temperatures as low as -50°C (-58°F).

Sea ice Antarctic

Penguins and **snow petrels** live in Antarctica. Penguins are the only birds that breed on sea ice, using it to slide into the ocean for food. Snow petrels perch on icebergs and islands, where they create nests made from pebbles.

Sea cliffs Antarctic

Birds such as the **Antarctic shag** nest in big sea cliff colonies in the Southern Ocean off the coast of Antarctica. They dive from the water surface to catch krill and squid.

Water Arctic

Nicknamed 'sea parrots', puffins spend most of their lives in the open ocean, paddling, resting, swimming, or diving.

Atlantic puffin

Cities

In cities, skyscrapers replace cliffs, trains criss-cross the ground, and millions of people live in small spaces. Most urban jungles are home to birds, but there is always more we can do to make them welcome.

Red-tailed hawk

Magnificent frigatebird

American robin

Red cardinal

Saffron finch

Toco toucan

New York, USA

Pockets of green spaces can serve as a great habitat for wildlife in cities. Pigeons, cardinals, and the American robin flourish in New York's Central Park – they just have to avoid the red-tailed hawk!

Rio de Janeiro, Brazil

Many of Rio's birds are as colourful as the city's famous Carnival. You can spot toco toucans and bright yellow saffron finches along with magnificent frigatebirds with their bright red chests.

London, UK

London is home to over 10 million people and 400 species of bird. Among them, the **ring-necked parakeet** – originally from South Asia – has learned to thrive, despite no one truly knowing how they got here!

Carrion crow

Akita, Japan

Crows are highly intelligent, especially with tools and problem-solving. In Akita, they have been seen to drop walnuts onto roads so cars drive over them and crack the shells, allowing the crows to swoop in and eat the nuts!

Tokyo, Japan

Only 8% of Tokyo is green space, but still there are over 700 species of bird living in the city. Japanese white-eyes and kingfishers can be seen flitting about the busiest city in the world.

Sydney, Australia

In Sydney, you can hear the laugh of the kookaburra, see pelicans resting on lampposts, and spot flocks of rainbow lorikeets splashing colour across the sky.

Rainforests

The world's dense, lush rainforests lie near the equator. Flashes of colourful plumages dart by every minute, and treetop canopies ring with melodic calls. Birds are kept busy hunting, pollinating plants, and munching on fruit and insects.

Scarlet macaw

Canopy

The canopy is a lively hub where most animals in the rainforest live. Parrots, jacamars, and many more birds inhabit this tier.

Understory

This understory is filled with shrubs and young trees that compete for sunlight in the shade of towering giants. Trogons and barbets fly very little, nesting in tree holes and feasting on insects and lizards.

Blue-throated barbet

Malayan peacock-pheasant

Forest floor

It's much darker on the forest floor than in the upper rainforest levels, so fewer plants grow. Birds such as the Malayan peacock-pheasant in Southeast Asia and the magnificent riflebird in Australia and New Guinea forage for seeds, fruits, and insects.

Emergent layer

This is the highest level of trees. Flying up here in the Amazon rainforest is the **harpy eagle**, believed to be the most powerful bird on earth. Its huge talons can even crush monkeys and sloths.

Rufous-tailed Jacamar

Bare-cheeked trogon

Magnificent riflebird

Myna birds hitch rides on elephants' backs, feeding on bugs that jump out when the elephant uproots plants. In return, the birds remove ticks and parasites from the elephants.

Mohican-haired turacos, found in dense African rainforests, are known for their bright green colour. They are the only bird with a truly green pigment in their feathers.

The **red junglefowl**, found in South and Southeast Asia, is the ancestor of domesticated chickens, which means that chickens surprisingly come from the rainforest!

What Do Birds Do?

Birds have different lifestyles. Social flamingos live in flocks, while kingfishers are solitary birds. Some birds migrate over long distances, while others stay in the same area year-round.

Andean flamingo

Flamingos flock together in the hundreds and even thousands by lakes, lagoons, and swamps, feeding on things like shrimp which turns their feathers pink. A group is known as a 'flamboyance of flamingos'!

Coupling Up

Around 90% of birds are socially monogamous – this means they have one mate at a time. Having two parents able to incubate the eggs and search for food helps the baby birds reach adulthood.

Laysan albatross

Enduring love

Albatrosses are true romantics, often forming lifelong bonds. Couples endure long separations when travelling huge distances across oceans, but they faithfully reunite at breeding grounds.

Lifelong bonds

Birds have fascinating love stories. Some birds pair up for life, finding remarkable ways to navigate it together.

Atlantic puffin

Mandarin duck

The majestic **bald eagle** forms an unbreakable bond with a single mate.

A bald eagle courtship dance is known as a 'cartwheel display'. The pair lock together their talons while in flight and spin like a tornado. They can stay in this daredevil embrace for hours – love truly is in the air!

Black-capped chickadee

Bald eagle couples work together to build and maintain their nests, and feed and protect their baby eaglets.

Grey-crowned crane

Killer Strategies

Given that birds come from dinosaurs, it's no surprise that many are brilliant hunters. There are lots of different tricks that birds employ to catch their dinner.

Herons

Herons are patient hunters. They can stand as still as a statue for hours waiting to strike, before jabbing a spear-like beak into fish in rivers and streams.

Grey heron

Shrike

Little impaler

Nicknamed 'the butcherbird', shrikes are small but brutal. They skewer insects, small rodents, and small birds on thorns... Ouch!

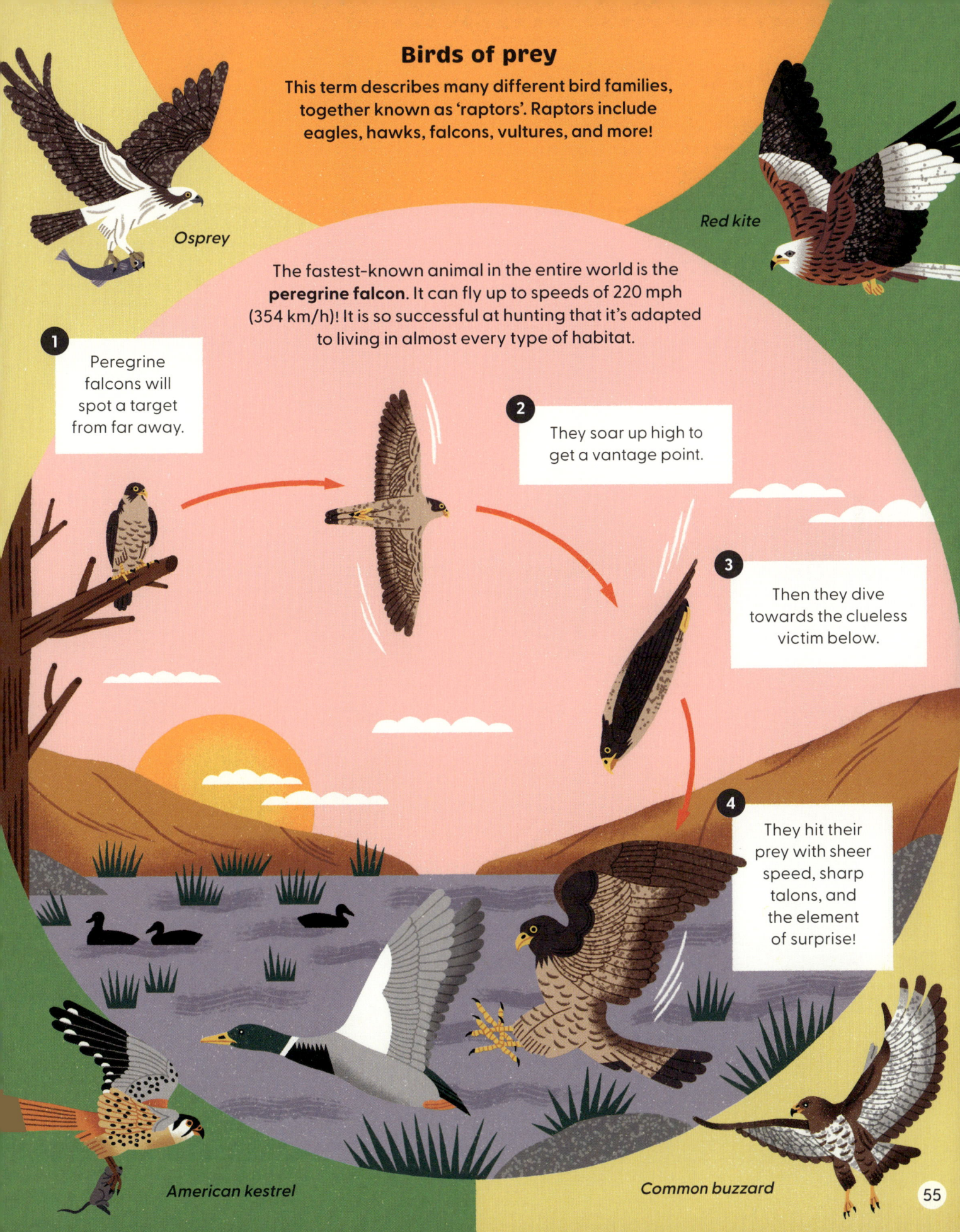

Epic Journeys

Migration is one of the wonders of the bird world: just how do they know where to go? Notice the birds around you — they may be visitors from the other side of the world!

Longest journey

The **Arctic tern** has the longest bird migration. They travel over 88,500 km (55,000 miles) from the North Pole to the South Pole every year, and can even eat and sleep while flying!

Hollow bones

The wandering bird

The biggest flying bird is the **wandering albatross**. It can travel over oceans as far as the distance between London and Sydney.

Long-distance migrations

From the Arctic to the tropics, these feathered globetrotters go on epic adventures over tens of thousands of miles.

In 2022, a tiny five-month-old **bar-tailed godwit** set the world record for the longest non-stop bird migration of 13,560 km (8,425 miles). This journey took 11 days and one hour, from Alaska to Tasmania.

Baltimore oriole

Painted bunting

Pied flycatcher

Sooty shearwater

Arctic tern

FACT FILE
Navigation

Around 50% of birds migrate. Seabirds, songbirds, and raptors share flyways across the world, going north to south and back again.

Bar-headed geese can reach heights of 8 km (4.97 miles) above sea level when migrating over the world's tallest mountains, the Himalayas.

Homing pigeons are known for using impeccable navigation skills to find their way back home. During the First and Second World Wars, they delivered important letters that were tied to their legs.

Warblers, along with other songbirds, opt for night-time migrations, as there is less risk of being dehydrated from the Sun's heat.

White storks have formed lifelong bonds with humans in countries such as Türkiye and Serbia, returning yearly to nest in the same chimneys and gardens.

Thanks to bird feeders in UK gardens, some populations of blackcap now migrate from Europe to the UK for the winter!

Eurasian blackcap warbler

Nesting

From master weavers to mud architects, birds have invented practical, genius, and strange methods for building homes to raise the next generation.

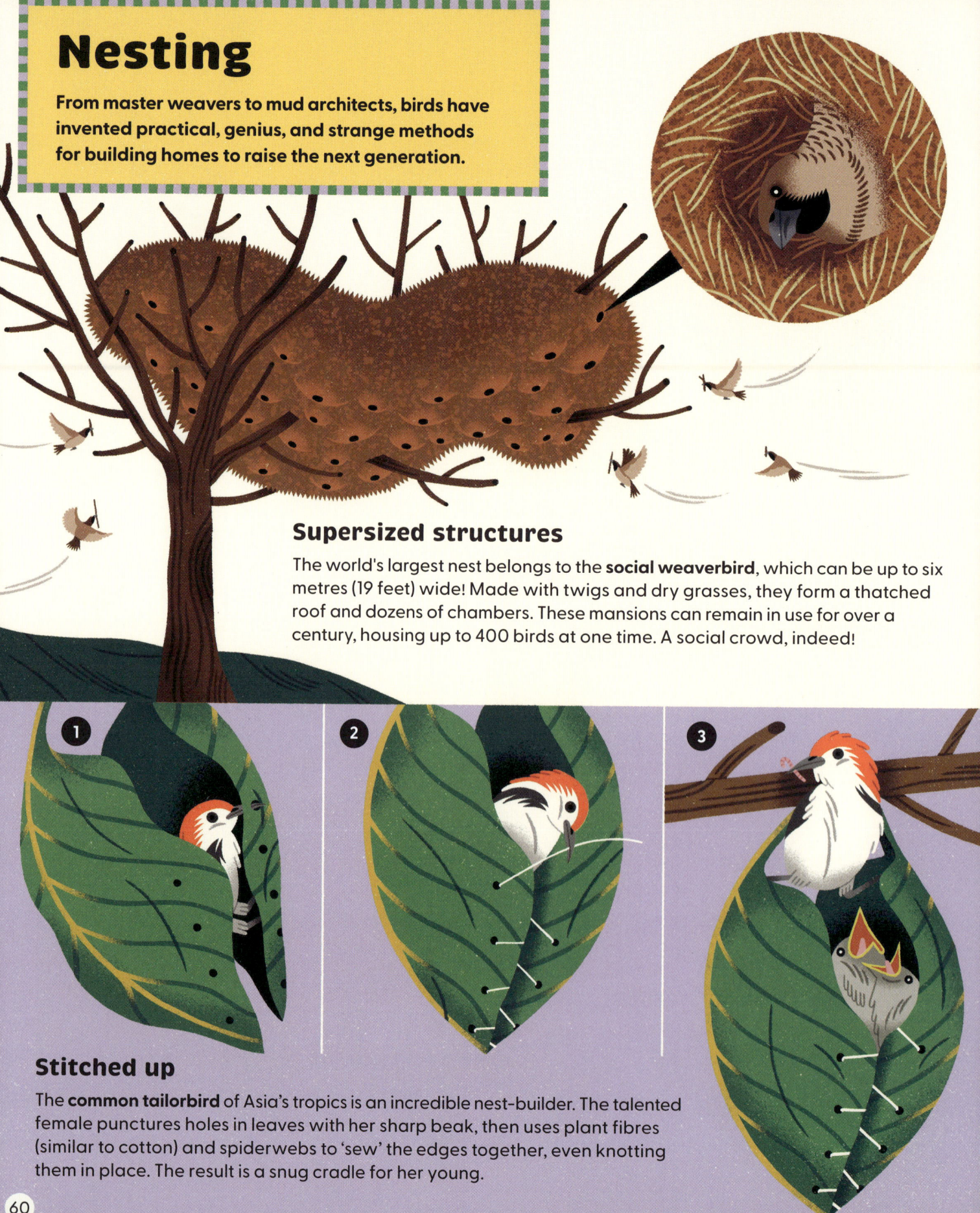

Supersized structures

The world's largest nest belongs to the **social weaverbird**, which can be up to six metres (19 feet) wide! Made with twigs and dry grasses, they form a thatched roof and dozens of chambers. These mansions can remain in use for over a century, housing up to 400 birds at one time. A social crowd, indeed!

Stitched up

The **common tailorbird** of Asia's tropics is an incredible nest-builder. The talented female punctures holes in leaves with her sharp beak, then uses plant fibres (similar to cotton) and spiderwebs to 'sew' the edges together, even knotting them in place. The result is a snug cradle for her young.

Red ovenbird

Gila woodpecker

Unusual roosts

Birds can, and do, make themselves right at home in the most unexpected places.

Edible-nest swiftlets are small birds found in Southeast Asia, who have a peculiar talent of building nests made almost entirely of their own saliva!

The birds build these nests in secluded, damp, dark spaces – from caves to clifftops. Their saliva hardens and sticks to the rocky walls, like drool cement. Pretty gross!

Some nests are farmed to make a highly prized and extremely expensive dish: bird's nest soup.

Megapode

Baya weaver

FACT FILE
Nests

Birds build nests to raise young, and so they have to be as safe, camouflaged, and sheltered as possible – all tough things to achieve in the unpredictable natural world.

Cuckoos have found a sneaky way to get free babysitters. They lay their eggs in another bird's nest, tricking them into raising the chicks as their own!

Redstart

Young cuckoo

Cuckoo's egg

Kingfishers dig their own nest tunnels, sometimes structuring them with regurgitated fish bones!

European bee-eaters excavate burrows in the sides of riverbanks, returning to nest after catching insects in flight.

Peregrine numbers are on the up in cities such as London and New York, as skyscrapers and bridges have become their adopted homes.

Coots nest on anything they can find along rivers and canals – from narrowboats to floating buoys.

Nature's Gardeners

Birds help shape the natural world by pollinating plants and spreading seeds. When they feed, they carry seeds and pollen as they flit away, helping new plants grow.

Pink-headed fruit dove

Orange fruit dove

Many-coloured fruit dove

Rose-crowned fruit dove

Superb fruit dove

Fruit farmers

There are over 50 kinds of fruit doves, and they love eating fruit! By dropping seeds (in their poo!), they help grow new trees and keep forests healthy.

Flower power

Some birds have a sweet tooth! They use their tiny, curved beaks to sip the sweet nectar from a flower, before zipping off to find more treats.

Hummingbirds beat their wings about 80 times per second and have hearts that pump 1,200 times per minute! This helps them to hover and feed as often as possible on their favourite food – nectar from flowers.

Because of how much energy they need for flying, hummingbirds can travel up to 40 km (24.85 miles) in a day, moving from flower to flower.

Ruby-throated hummingbird

Hummingbirds love bright pink and red flowers, especially ones with tubes holding lots of tasty nectar, like trumpet creepers.

The **Anna's hummingbird** is common along America's west coast. It thrives living alongside humans.

Sunbird

Spiderhunter sunbird

Honeyeater

Flowerpecker

Honeycreeper

Flowerpiercer

Rainbow lorikeet

White-eye

Green wood hoopoe

Tūī

Night Vision

Nocturnal birds rule the realms of the dark night until sunrise. Their night vision and excellent hearing make this the ideal time for them to hunt.

Barn owl

Masters of the night

Owls have big, powerful eyes. If owls were human-sized, their eyes would be the size of grapefruits! They see well at night due to reflective layers in their eyes, and are experts at spotting movement in the dark.

Becoming a Birder

Birding, or birdwatching, is easier than you might think. With the right steps, you can spot, identify, and help care for the birds around you.

My birding journey: Nadeem

When I started birding, I had no idea what to look out for. I hadn't studied birds, and most of the time I wouldn't know what species I was looking at. So if you want to get into birding, but you don't know about all the birds we've looked at in this book, I'm here to tell you not to worry!

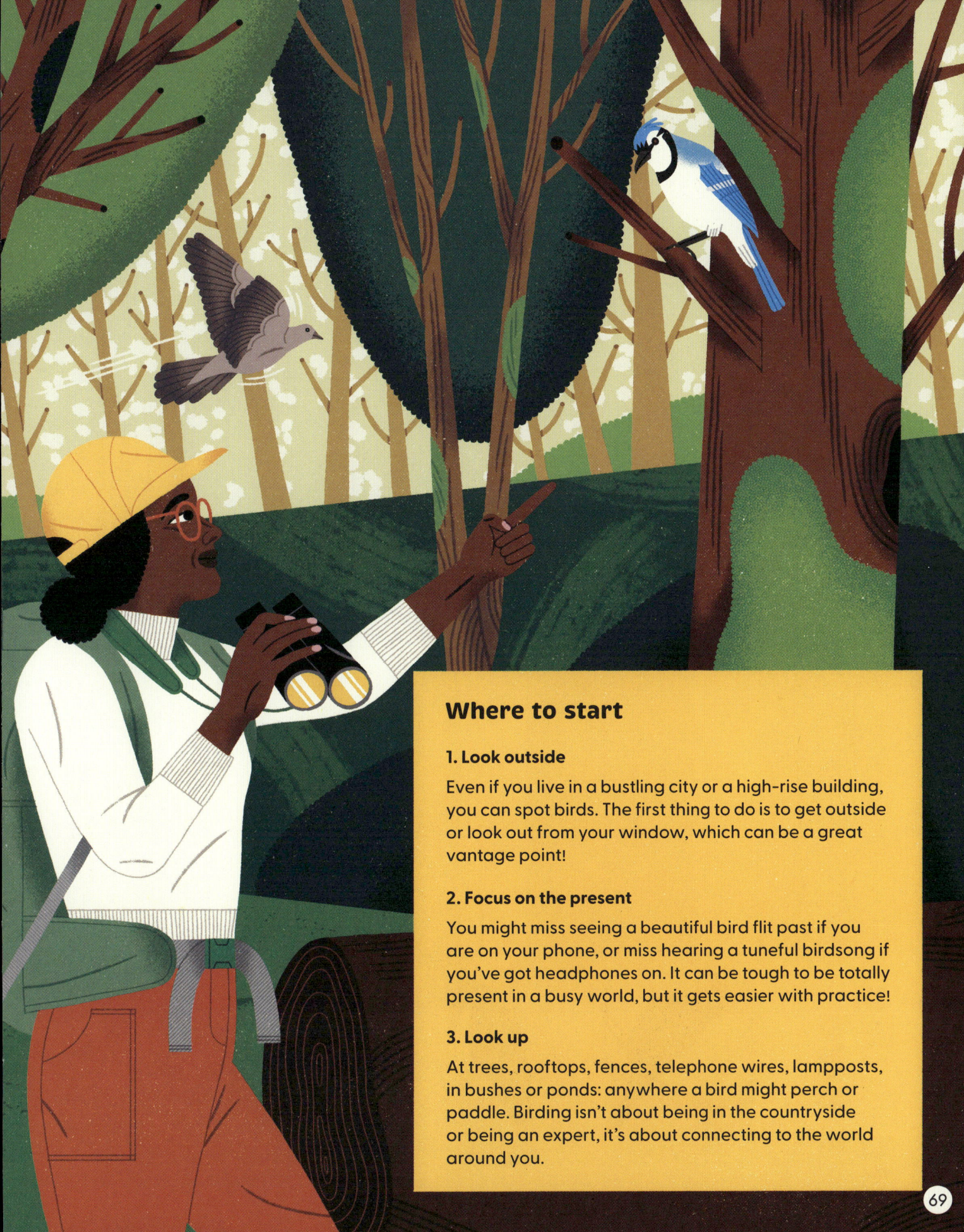

Where to start

1. Look outside
Even if you live in a bustling city or a high-rise building, you can spot birds. The first thing to do is to get outside or look out from your window, which can be a great vantage point!

2. Focus on the present
You might miss seeing a beautiful bird flit past if you are on your phone, or miss hearing a tuneful birdsong if you've got headphones on. It can be tough to be totally present in a busy world, but it gets easier with practice!

3. Look up
At trees, rooftops, fences, telephone wires, lampposts, in bushes or ponds: anywhere a bird might perch or paddle. Birding isn't about being in the countryside or being an expert, it's about connecting to the world around you.

Cheerful, fast-paced twittering melody

What kind of sound did it make?

Did it make a warbling sound, a high-pitched trill, or a raspy caw? Is it the same melody repeated, or is it a short burst of sound?

What was it doing?

This question will really help to whittle down the species. Bird behaviour tends to suit the environment they live in.

Kestrels hover by facing the wind, adjusting their wings and tails to stay in place. In a breeze, they seem still, but on calm days, they flap faster. This helps them carefully scan the ground to spot scurrying rodents.

Twists and turns when in flight

So what was our bird?

A European goldfinch

Now you have all the information you need to make an entry in your bird log!

Male mandarin duck

Female mandarin duck

Often, males have more colourful a plumage used to attract mates, while females are more camouflage, which helps when nesting and looking after young.

Make a Bird Log

Make your own bird log! Keep a notebook or some paper near your favourite birdwatching spot and note down any details when you spot one. Logging these details will help you learn more about the birds when you get a chance to research them!

Step 1: Time and place

Note the time and location of the sighting. Is the bird most active in the morning? It is going back and forth feeding its young in a tree cavity? Like us, birds are active at different times and have habitat likes and dislikes.

Step 2: Size

Start by noting physical details. If a golden eagle is large and a robin is small, how big is the bird you've just seen? Small? Medium? Small-medium?

Step 3: Plumage

Are the head feathers a different colour to its body? Are its chest feathers patterned? Are its feathers soft or with a metallic sheen? Note the colour, patterns, and textures of the bird's feathers.

Step 4: Sounds

Write down the kind of chirp, whistle, shriek or hoot you can hear. Is it the same melody repeated, or is it a short burst of sound?

Step 5: Bird behaviour

Did the bird fly, feed, or hop about? Did it swoop, hover or twist and turn in the air? If it was eating, what was it – seeds, fruit, or scavenging? Was it alone or with a group of other birds – if so, how many?

Step 6: Research

Visit a library, and read a bird book, or use a search engine to research. For example, you could search 'small brown bird in North America with an orange chest'.

Take it further

You could get some binoculars, a pocket-sized guidebook, and ask an adult to download a free bird identifier app. You can join birding communities online or in person, and check out resources at the British Trust for Ornithology, RSPB, Audubon, BirdLife International, and the Great Backyard Bird Count.

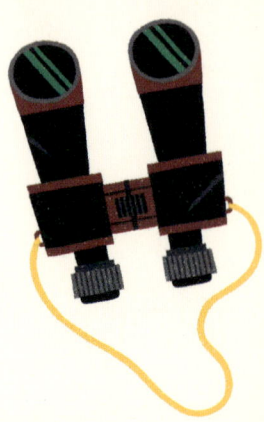

Birdwatching Logbook

Bird species   **Date:**   **Time:**

Season: ◯ Winter   ◯ Spring   ◯ Summer   ◯ Autumn

Location: *where did you see them?*

Size:

Small ◯ ─── ◯ ─── ◯ ─── ◯ ─── ◯ Large

Plumage: *what do their feathers look like?*

Colour:

Chest	Wings	Head

Sound:

◯ Chirp   ◯ Whistle   ◯ Shriek   ◯ Hoot   ◯ Melody   ◯ Repeated   ◯ Single burst

Behaviour: *what are they doing?*

How You Can Help

As hard as birds tirelessly work towards the success of their species, they still face a struggling future. Deforestation, pollution, and climate change are threats to our feathered friends, but the good news is that small, everyday actions can go a long way.

Food and water

The easiest way to help birds is to provide food and water. You can make bird feeders and baths from recycled materials like plastic bottles and cups. There are also feeders that stick to your window! Remember to clean and move bird feeders to help stop the spread of diseases.

Plant life

Things that attract birds include insects, trees, and bushes filled with seeds and berries, and wildflowers and nectar-rich flowers. If you have outdoor space, you could install a bird box for nesting and a bird bath for resting and drinking.

Community

You could raise awareness and share your love of birds by starting a birdwatching club. I did this with a friend, and now we have a large group, TV show, and books dedicated to birds! A community fosters friendship, idea-sharing, and outdoor exploration, all priceless in today's fast-paced world.

How many ideas can you come up with to connect people with birds and the natural world? Everyone has the power to help make a real difference, in your garden, local community, country, and beyond!

Glossary

Adaptation – When a species evolves special features to improve its chances of survival

Aerodynamic – Evolved to move smoothly through the air with little resistance

Apex predator – Animals at the top of the food chain

Breeding ground – An environment where animals reproduce

Camouflage – An animal's appearance allowing them to blend in with their surroundings

Deforestation – The cutting down of large areas of trees

Ecosystem – The interaction between a community of living things and their environment

Extinction – When an entire species, or type, dies out

Fossils – The remains or traces of plants and animals that lived long ago

Habitat – A natural home for a living creature

Lagoon – A big, shallow pool of water separated from a larger body of water by land or coral reefs

Magnetic field – An invisible force created by forces inside of the earth

Migration – The movement of living things from one region to another, usually to find food, mates or warmer weather

Nocturnal – A creature that is most active at night and usually sleeps during the day

Permafrost – Ground that stays totally frozen for at least two years, typically near the Earth's North and South poles

Pollen – A substance produced by plants, allowing them to reproduce

Pollination – When pollen is transferred to the stigma of a flower by a pollinator (such as an insect or bird), the flower can be fertilised and turn into a fruit containing seeds

Pollution – Substances in the environment that can be harmful to living things. If something has too much pollution in it, it is called 'polluted'

Synchronised – Happening or moving together at the same time

Territory – The area an animal lives in, which they may defend from other animals

Therapod – Dinosaurs that walked on two legs, mostly carnivorous like *Tyrannosaurus rex* and *Velociraptor*

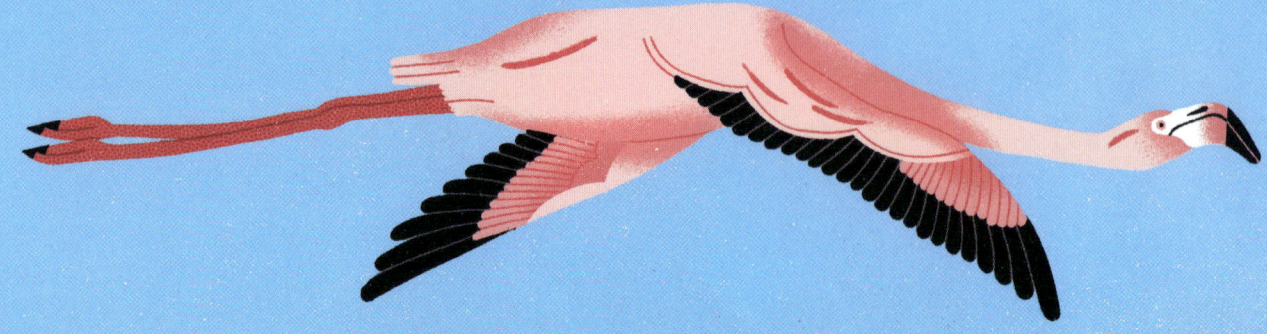

Bird Species Index

Albatross 35, 52, 56
    wandering 35, 56
Arctic redpoll 42
Arctic tern 56–7

Bar-tailed godwit 57
Barbet 48
Bee-eater 63
    European 63
Bird of paradise 21, 48
    magnificent riflebird 48
Blackbird 19, 39
    Baltimore oriole 57
Blue jay 20
Blue tit 25
Bowerbird 21
Budgerigar (budgie) 25
Bulbul 36
Buzzard 38, 55
    common 55

Canary 19
Cardinal 44
    red 44
    painted bunting 57
Cassowary 17
Chickadee 38, 53
    black-capped 53
Coot 63
Crane 13, 53
    grey-crowned 53
    sandhill 13
Crossbill 29
Crow 45
    jay 20, 40
    raven 36
    magpie 25, 70
Cuckoo 62
    roadrunner 40

Dove 47, 64
    rock 47
    superb fruit 64
Duck 28, 53, 71
    Australasian shoveler 28
    mandarin 53, 71

Eagle 24, 37, 49, 53, 55, 72
    bald 53
    golden 37, 72
    harpy 49
Emu 17

Falcon 36, 47, 55
    falconet 36
    peregrine 47, 55
Finch 19, 28, 44
    Genovesa cactus 28
    gold 19
    green warbler 28
    house 19
    large ground 28
    saffron 44
Flamingo 50–1
Flowerpecker 65
Flowerpiercer 65
Flycatcher 57
    pied 57
Frigatebird 21, 44
Frogmouth 22
    Tawny 22
Fulmar 35

Goldfinch 19, 71
    European 71
Goose 14–5, 58
    bar-headed 58
    barnacle 15
    Canada 14
Goshawk 38–9
Grandala 36

Hawk 27, 44, 55
    red-tailed 44
Heron 54
    grey 54
Hoatzin 13
Honeyeater 65
Hoopoe 40, 65
    green wood 65
Hornbill 33
    great 33
Hummingbird 8, 40–1, 65
    Anna's 65
    Black-chinned 41
    Cuban bee 8–9

Jacamar 48
Jay 40, 45
    Mongolian ground 40
Junglefowl 49

Kākāpō 17
Kestrel 25, 55, 71
    American 55
    common 25
Kingfisher 46, 50, 63
Kite 38, 55
    red 55
Kiwi 17
Kookaburra 46

Lark 19
    skylark 19
Long-billed curlew 29

Macaw 27, 48
    scarlet 48
Magpie 25, 70
    Australian 25
Megapode 61
Mockingbird 19
Myna 49

Nightjar 27

Oilbird 67
Osprey 55
Ostrich 13
    African 13
Ovenbird 61
    red 61
Owl 23, 26, 36, 41, 66
    barn 26
    burrowing 26, 41
    great horned 26
    Himalayan wood 36
    short-eared 23, 26
    tawny 38
    white 36

Parakeet 45
    ring-necked 45
Parrot 25, 27, 31, 48, 65
    African grey 25
    panama Amazon 31
    rainbow lorikeet 65
    scarlet macaw 27
Peafowl 21
    peacock 21
    peahen 21
Pelican 30, 46
    American white 30
Penguin 16–7, 20, 32, 35, 42
    adélie 42
    gentoo 20
    king 35
Pheasant 48
    Malayan peacock 48
Pigeon 32, 44, 47, 59
    homing 59
Potoos 27
Puffin 16, 43
    Atlantic 43, 53

Roadrunner 40
Robin 18–9, 39, 44, 72
    American 39, 44
    European 18, 71
Ruff 21

Shearwater 34, 57
    Manx 34
    sooty 57
Shoveler 28
    Australasian 28
Shrike 54
Snow petrel 42
Sparrow 19, 46
    House 19
Spoonbill 29
Starling 15
    European 15
Stork 15, 59, 71
    white 15, 59, 71
    black 71
Sunbird 65
Swallow 15
Swan 23
    cygnet 23
Swift 14, 61, 67
    common 14
    edible-nest 61
    swiftlet 61, 67

Tailorbird 60
    common 60
Thrush 19
    groundscraper 19
Tit 25, 70
    blue 25
Toucan 29, 31, 44
    toco 31, 44
Treecreeper 38
Trogon 48
Tūī 65
Turaco 49

Vulture 37, 41, 55
    bearded 37
    rüppell's 41

Wallcreeper 32, 37
Warbler 59
    blackcap 59
Waxwing 15, 38
    bohemian 15
Weaver 60, 61
    baya 61
    social 60
White-eye 46, 65
    Japanese 46
Woodpecker 29, 31, 38–9, 61
    gila 61
    great spotted 29
    green 39
    pileated 31
Wren 39, 70
    Eurasian 39

Written by Nadeem Perera

Nadeem Perera is a wildlife TV presenter, author, and activist. He is the co-founder of the birdwatching collective Flock Together, which encourages people of colour to get out, enjoy nature, and support each other. Born and raised in London, Nadeem's love of nature expressed itself at an early age when it helped him to overcome mental roadblocks and trauma. He has appeared on the BBC's *Springwatch*, *Winterwatch*, *The One Show*, and CBBC's *One Zoo Three Goes Wild in Britain*.

Illustrated by Montse Galbany

Montse Galbany started drawing as soon as she could hold a pencil and has never stopped since. She is an illustrator and graphic designer living in Granollers, a city close to Barcelona, Spain. She studied graphic design at Elisava University and has been working as an illustrator since 2017. She works digitally with friendly shapes and vibrant colours to tell stories. She has been published by Rebel Girls, Penguin Random House, and Editorial Planeta, among others.